I0802461

WE FALL LIKE CHILDREN

XHEVDET BAJRAJ

Translations from Albanian and Spanish
by Ani Gjika and Alice Whitmore

Egret

CHAPEL HILL
2018

Copyright © 2000, 2015, 2016, and 2017 by Xhevdet Bajraj
Translation copyright (from the Albanian) © 2018 by Ani Gjika
Translation copyright (from the Spanish) © 2016 and 2018 by Alice Whitmore

ALL RIGHTS RESERVED

First Edition

Printed in the United States of America

Cover and book design by Maxine Mills

"The Angel and the Ex Angels" and "The Shopping Bag" first appeared in *Seizure*, www.seizureonline.com. Reprinted with kind permission.

Laertes

Egret is an imprint of Laertes Press, Incorporated | www.laertesbooks.org

SCRIPT

Throughout the long drama of life
in the land of perfumeless flowers
he had an easy job
he played the part of a dead man

—AW

THE REFUGEE'S SUITCASE

You took
the phone numbers of the dead
rivers mountains hills
the sky above your motherland
love
and fear
all inside a plastic bag
and arrived in a new place
to live free
forever
inside the pupil of the assassin's eye
that watches you
through a crosshair

—*AG*

TORTILLA CHIP

The world appears so much better off
when you close your eyes
but how can I stop this blazing fire
that blooms inside me

I'm not from here or from over there
with my fingers I lift a tortilla chip
dipped in rancid fear
and spicy habanero sauce
which remind me
that beauty
can still make me cry

(Life has taught me
that this world is better seen
with eyes closed
the way we do when we kiss
or when we're kissed
by death)

—*AG*

PORTRAIT OF A CHILD AT THE WINDOW

The history of civilization
is equal to the bleating of the sheep
that runs after her little lamb
at the slaughter

And a child looks at all this
from a window to nowhere

—*AG*

AMONG THE RUINS

From the ruins
a whole new city may be built
but all I could possibly manage
is to bloom like a flower
on some destroyed wall
and wait to turn red
when she gets close enough
to smell me

—*AG*

THE SHOT

A shot echoes
in the forest of alternate spaces
It rips apart the head of a bird
that while falling
penetrates the dream
of a fevered child
who cries
shivers
begins to sweat
outstretches his arms
but doesn’t flap them

because he never wakes up

—*AG*

THE BOOK OF THE DEAD

The wind
of the saltless sea of memory
flips the pages of *The Book of the Dead*

In front of our eyes
wither from loneliness
flowers plucked in the name of love

On our deaf ears
dangle like earrings the songs of birds
whose names we've long forgotten

Inside the transparent walls of a dream
the sun rots
like an apple

—*AG*

WE FALL LIKE CHILDREN

The echo of footsteps that fled
whitens our hair
darkened
by the slime of a Balkan animal

On city streets
we fall like children
and get up like old people
just to mark our nameless graves

It's not dark yet
but bats fly
after the scent of stale blood
a masked herd leaves behind

In the heart of the city
donkeys graze and copulate
under a sky laden with butterflies
multiplying along our graves

—AG

FLOWER OF THE SOUL

A woman

young and beautiful

black scarf wreathing her head

looks into the mirror

she does not recognise herself

Pain

the flower of the soul

clouds her view

—*AW*

THE DOLL

Although the occupation army has retreated from the city
a six-year-old girl
takes up her doll
that's missing one leg
and with her open palm shuts the doll's eyes

—*AG*

CLOTHES FOR MY PAIN

The cold night has a beast's hunger
You are distant
resting there on the bed of the Great Dream
solitude goes quietly through your veins
and you breathe yearning like air
I
with slender threads of night
stitch thoughts
into clothes for my pain
You and I, father
we measure ourselves with death
you and I…
Outside someone is crying out
outside someone is crying
Great God
they're killing us again

—*AW*

PEACE

I watch TV with my head on the pillow
stuffed with the feathers of nine angels
To the little mouse who calmly grazes
on the crumbs of my morning
I pitch the apple that evicted us from paradise
and rest again my head
on the pillow stuffed
with the feathers of nine angels
With the bedroom window closed
I can shut out the world
I change the channel
hear the news say:
After the expulsion of Serbian forces from Kosovo
eight hundred Albanians were killed in Civil War…
I rest again my head on the pillow stuffed
with the feathers of nine angels
I'm keeping
the redblack flag
they will hang it on my tomb

I smile to myself
and from the tabletop
the worm inside the broken apple
smiles at me
Where to turn my head but to the pillow
stuffed with the feathers of nine angels
Rifle shots from the neighbour's house
then a cry
two cries three
weeping
only cries and weeping
and the footfalls of men with masked faces
Suddenly I'm cold
I bury my head under the pillow
stuffed with the feathers of nine angels
and cover my body with the quilt
stuffed with the down of ninety-nine angels
and I rest
in peace

—*AW*

ABSOLUTE TRUTH

Absolute truth is

a naked man

and a naked woman

in bed

—*AW*

ONCE AND NOW

She sleeps exhausted dreaming of the days when we
  consumed bread and hope
and on the sky above each day the sun dangled blind
  by its own light
The smell of roses would enter through the open window
  of our library room
while I wrote poems about days that never arrived
I'd wait for you with a bottle of wine on the table
and a lit candle
yes
the world was colorful

When the sun would fall like a rotten apple
and the stars burnt around mother moon
we made love while crickets sang
a song older than mankind

Then war snatched away the life we had
we discovered how wonderful it is to lose your job
to get stuck at home or go outside
without knowing where you're headed or what you'll do

We discovered that breaking an arm or a leg
means you are alive
that life is beautiful
bitter and beautiful when freely lived

Now we have a library with nearly all the same books again
but in a different language
in a different language I write lines about the days that will
  never come back
in a different language I seek for bread at a bakery
in a different language my love
now
life hurts

—*AG*

LOOK AT ME

When you're left alone
and the black waters are foaming at the door of your life
go outside, find a cantina
and after the seventh or eighth drink
the only thing you'll feel is missing
will be a bowl of salted peanuts

Look at me
I am happy
between the first and third coffee
that is
for approximately one and a half hours
each day

—AW

THE ANGEL AND THE EX ANGELS

The angel came down from heaven to the five-star hotel
Descended to the ground floor in the elevator
Entered the WC of the nocturnal bar
Urinated hastily
Calmly snorted cocaine
(up on high, discipline is iron-clad)
When he returned to the bar
With injected eyes he discovered the secret
That all of us are angels
Expelled from paradise

—AW

THE SHOPPING BAG

I don't know about you, dear friend
but life keeps biting me with its beastly teeth
and there's nothing left to do
but bite back

I flick away my cigarette and cross the street patiently
so that some car doesn't tear off
            my brand new shoes

I walk into the supermarket
lamb chops
a selection of fish
chicken wings breasts thighs… whole chickens
bull testicles cow brains beef liver
pig trotters rabbits quails
all heavy, all carefully packaged
with the price in the corner
to see if we can afford it

I carry a bag with tortillas

green chiles

six Indio beers, nice and cold

three packets of Delicados, no filter

and I return home

to eat

tortillas with chile

and a little piece of myself

—AW

WRISTBONES

The bleeding dove came into the cage of the chest
I slake my thirst in the river
that runs now only in memory
and crawl out through the black holes of the brain
Above the flowers of the brow
that bloomed against the graves
the dawn dances, naked-bellied and chiming
On her ankles, shining bracelets
fashioned from the bones of our wrists
and inscribed with the initials
of our friends
I'm dying, hear? I'm dying of a hunger
for your living, Kosovo
for your dead
Oh well...
the ones who write the sweetest lines
the ones who sing most sweetly
are those unafraid to live in death

—AW

EXILED

Roughly a hundred and fifty meters away from a brook
near the place I was born
on a cliff
wild doves dwelt

When they flew
over the grand rock
God descended

Much later I came to understand that He walked with us
once
only to abandon us when we went on getting older

From there
In the cabin of a plane-crucifix
I took the long way around the world
searching for rocks to build a house

And I've gathered nearly all of them

but

where will I raise the walls of the house

what views will I capture inside window frames

to find the way back to childhood

—*AG*

THE FLOWERS

Flowers

when they are born

cry

like babies

—*AW*

The following poems were taken from the anthology, *My Own Shred of Sky*, published in 2015:

Script

Tortilla Chip

Among the Ruins

The Book of the Dead

We Fall like Children

Flower of the Soul

Clothes for my Pain

Peace

Absolute Truth

Once and Now

Look at Me

Wristbones

Exiled

The Flowers

These poems were taken from the anthology, *Rose Water*, published in 2017:

The Refugee's Suitcase

Portrait of a Child at the Window

The Shot

The Doll

The Angel and the Ex Angels first appeared in *Ruego Albanés*, published in 2000.

Shopping Bag first appeared in *Sueños*, published in 2016.